CONSTABULAR DUTIES

A History of Policing in Picture Postcards

by

Michael V. Dixon

Foreword by Sir Peter Imbert, Q.P.M.
Commissioner of the Metropolitan Police

S. B. Publications
1990

Dedicated to my wife, Jillian, in appreciation of her support in producing this book.

First published in 1990 by S. B. Publications
5 Queen Margaret's Road, Loggerheads, Nr. Market Drayton, Shropshire, TF9 4EP.

ISBN 1 870708 43 1

Typeset and printed by Geo. R. Reeve Ltd., Wymondham, Norfolk NR18 0BD.

British Library Cataloguing in Publication Data
Constabulary Duties: a history of policing in picture postcards.
1. Great Britain. Police, history
I. Dixon, Michael V.
365.20941

ISBN 1-870708-43-1

CONTENTS

CONTENTS CONTINUED

CONTENTS CONTINUED

ACKNOWLEDGEMENTS

It is with appreciation that I acknowledge the assistance given by the following people and police forces in providing photographic material or research information:-

Richard Sharp – Metropolitan Police Museum, pages 1, 4, 42,44, 45, 50.
Ray Hayter, City of London Police Museum, page 60.
Supt. Brian Butcher, Norfolk Constabulary, pages 7, 66, 86, 90, 92.
Supt. R. Rees, Brecon, page 34.
Philip Standley, page 48.
Bessie Sewell, page 47.
Keith Pattison, pages 15, 75.
Tony Parkes, M.B.E., page 17.
Denis Williams, M.B.E., page 74.
Ben Pountain, M.B.E., page 16.
J/V Publications, page 93.
Pompadour Gallery, Romford, page 3.
Mike Englefield, Basingstoke Gazette, pages 56, 114.

BIBLIOGRAPHY

The Policeman's Lot – Antique British Police Equipment including Truncheons by Mervyn Mitton, published by Quilter Press Ltd.

Police Procedure, Administration and Organisation by J.D. Devlin, published by Butterworth, Ltd.

FOREWORD

by
Sir Peter Imbert, Q.P.M.
The Commissioner of the Metropolis

In this age of rapid communication and high technology it is difficult to appreciate the great progress that has been made over the past 160 years since the formation of the 'New Police'. We are therefore indebted to the inventor of the postcard who, inadvertently, provided such a wealth of police history without which many glimpses of early policing would have vanished. Michael Dixon has used his collection of postcards on the police in a fascinating and interesting way to illustrate the development of the police service.

Not only is one aware of the variations in uniform and duties, but also of the little known fact that the fire and ambulance services were first vested in the police or that the first policemen wore high leather collars to prevent garotting. As the policeman became accepted by the populace his role was expanded and he became recognised as the helpful face of authority, the one person to whom anyone could turn. Some things have not materially changed – policing a major disturbance or trade dispute was as onerous in 1911 as it is today and the sacrifices made in the course of duty bear witness to the professionalism and moral strength of police, both men and women, over the years.

I am pleased to endorse this historical record which graphically shows in all its aspects the constant service given by the police of Great Britain and I pay tribute to the dedication of policemen and policewomen past and present. One is left wondering how constabulary duties will change over the next century and a half.

INTRODUCTION

Postcards were first published in Great Britain on the 1st October, 1870. These were plain official cards produced by the Post Office and were used extensively for business purposes. It was not until 1894 that the first picture postcards were permitted whereby the picture and a message were allowed on one side with the address only on the reverse. These postcards were known as Court Cards and were smaller in size to those used elsewhere in the world. By 1902 the larger card, as we know it today, was accepted and the Post Office regulations allowed for the picture to cover one complete side and for the address and message to be on the other. These changes opened up the market and progressed the popularity of the picture postcard.

The 'Golden Age' of the postcard spanned a period of approximately 20 years at the start of this century. This was the period of the halfpenny postal rate and the publication of a varied and vast choice of cards depicting every subject and covering every taste imaginable.

Collecting became a national hobby; a craze encouraged by the publishers with competitions and prizes for those with the largest collection of their postcards. Every household had its own album of cards proudly available for all to peruse. The very nature of a families' position in society and their interests would be reflected in their collection and it is this wide variety of subject matter that makes postcard collecting just as fascinating today as then.

Postcards themselves can be loosely catagorised under three types – real photographic, sepia printed or colour printed. The colour process being used for the majority of art, greeting and subject cards. In the early years the bulk of coloured cards, although published by British companies such as Raphael Tuck, W.W. Faulkner or Stewart & Woolf, were printed in Germany. In particular the chromo-lithograph printing was superb and has not been surpassed to this day. Following the outbreak of war in 1914 items of German origin were frowned upon and postcards proudly declared their British manufacture.

Real photographic cards are of topographical interest being views of towns and villages, royal occasions and local events, all of which illustrate and provide a comprehensive record and social history of importance to local historians. The photographs were mostly taken by locally based photographers who published the cards in small numbers and these are now avidly sought by collectors.

The Edwardian policeman was respected and held a unique place in society, however judged by the numerous comic cards published he was also the butt of a host of humorous asides. This book concentrates on showing the development and role of the police service through photographic postcards of policemen going about their 'Constabulary Duties'.

Having been an avid collector of postcards for 28 years and a police officer in the Metropolitan Police and Norfolk Constabulary for a total of 32 years it is with pleasure that I have combined the two interests and formulated this historical portrait of the police.

Michael V. Dixon
Norwich
April, 1990

THE ORIGINS AND HISTORY OF POLICING

To find the origins of policing in Great Britain one has to go back 1100 years to the Saxon times with its preventative system based on the family.

The Saxons had instigated a tribal system of mutual pledging where the headman and members of each settlement were answerable to each other. This bond was used to maintain the peace in the locality. In addition, by swearing allegiance and good conduct to the King, the subjects in return received the all embracing security and protection of the "King's Peace" a term that is retained to the present day.

During the reign of Alfred the Great (870–901) the country was divided into shires or counties under the control of an appointed Earl who was responsible for the peace of his county. He had a functionary known as a Shire-reeve or Sheriff to assist him in that task. The family system was further refined with all freemen over twelve having to give their own individual pledge to uphold the law. They were grouped into 'Tithings' being ten families who were in turn combined into unions of ten being 100 families and known as a 'Hundred'. The term 'Hundred' survived to describe local authority administrative areas and as Petty Sessional Divisions for Courts of Law. This was a successful preventative system of self policing where all were reponsible and had to raise the 'Hue and Cry', band together and pursue any fleeing criminal.

After the Norman Conquest in 1066 the Saxon method of self policing became part of the Norman feudal system with the Norman Lords of the Manor taking over the policing responsibility from the Earls. The Sheriffs became the King's representatives collecting taxes, goods or money in what was generally an oppressive period. Henry I (1100–1135) had greater foresight and restored the earlier system and sent out justices or judges to try cases thereby bringing the crown back into contact with the people. The system remained with varying degrees of success over the years being dependant upon the attitude of the succeeding Kings. In many cases the citizens of towns and boroughs persevered with the system of mutual pledging for their own protection; the word "borough" stemming from an Anglo-Saxon word meaning defence and safety by those with a common purpose.

During this period Knights, being respected men, were appointed to try cases and punish law breakers and were the forerunners of the Justice of the Peace, today's magistrate. The position of Constable was also established, the word derives from the Latin 'comes-stabuli', meaning master of the horse. The name became interchangeable with that of Headman, being the person responsible for ensuring the peace was kept in a settlement or parish. Without such a constable a settlement could not be termed a parish. In 1272 Edward I came to the throne and in 1285 introduced the Statute of

Winchester which set defined principles of policing. It decreed that Hundreds would be answerable for all offences committed, that Sheriffs would reintroduce the hue and cry and that a new measure of 'Watch and Ward' would be introduced in towns and boroughs. To provide security town gates would be shut from sunset to sunrise with watchmen appointed to guard the gates. The watch and ward extended to London which was divided into 24 wards each controlled by an alderman. The watchmen had power to arrest criminals and take them before the Mayor for a hearing.

As policing evolved over the next 300 years the Saxon system made way for that based on the parish constable and Justice of the Peace. It should be born in mind that the constable was still the person responsible for ensuring that those people in his parish kept the law by the means of all having a bounden duty to assist in its upkeep and to arrest offenders when necessary. It is at this time when men were first paid to carry out the policing function and as all citizens were required to take their turn at policing it became common practice for the task to be delegated by paying others to do their work. Unfortunately those paid were often old, infirm, unsuitable and poorly paid, consequently in many places policing became discredited.

Following a short period of military rule and policing under Cromwell the appointment of parish constables was invested in Justices of the Peace and the start of an association that remains to this day. In cities the civil authority controlled the paid watchmen and in the event of an emergency could request the Justices to appoint a force of constables.

By 1750 London had its 'Charleys', the parish nightwatchman and a number of constables. In addition, Henry Fielding, a Police Magistrate, had become so concerned with the high incidence of crime that he raised money to pay for a force of men, known as the 'Bow Street Horse and Foot Patrol', to patrol the streets and for twelve 'Bow Street Runners' who were appointed to detect crime. They vainly worked to stem the level of rising crime and violence in London and were, to a degree, successful. As a result in 1792 the policing format spread throughout the County of Middlesex there being seven new police areas each with three magistrates and six constables.

During this period the word "police" became associated with the maintenance of law and order. The word stems from the Latin 'politia', and the Greek 'politeia', meaning the internal civil administration of a state for the protection of life and property, prevention of crime and offences and the preservation of law and order. These remain as the primary duties of every policeman.

In 1829 after long and considerable debate in Parliament, led by Sir Robert Peel and a great deal of opposition throughout the land because people feared loss of freedom, it was finally agreed there should be a new order of policing in London. An Act of Parliament was approved allowing for the Metropolitan Police to be formed. It can therefore be said that 1829 was the year in which the modern police service, of paid professional policemen, began.

Having proved their worth in London and having been accepted by the populace the demand for similar policing spread. In 1835 the Municipal Corporations Act required cities and boroughs to appoint a Watch Committee who were required by law to establish and maintain an adequate police force.

Within the rural counties the former system of parish constables being appointed by Justices remained. There was no co-ordination of control and the policing was often inefficient. The changes that had taken place in adjoining cities and boroughs had little effect on the rural areas.

This state could not continue and in 1839 the County Police Act gave Justices in Quarter Sessions the right to decide whether to establish a professional paid police force. In contrast to the city forces they were able to delegate powers to the Chief Constable who would then appoint, control and discipline the constables under his command. A few counties were progressive and immediately established a force, but sixteen years later only 28 rural forces had been formed. It then became compulsory and as a result from 1856 the whole of the country was for the first time policed by a paid professional force.

On the formation of the modern police one sees many features from the earlier systems of policing being preserved and to an extent retaining the principle that every citizen has a responsibility in maintaining law and order.

1) The new police retained the term constable and their powers were based on common law.
2) Control remained with Justices of the Peace and locally elected authorities who were responsible for maintaining a force. Today magistrates still provide one third of the membership of police authorities.
3) Constables were subject to the same laws as every citizen.
4) Constables acted as individuals being independent in enforcing the law but subject to internal discipline and lawful commands.

Over the years the system has evolved and been refined but the basic principles still hold good. The small forces were soon amalgamated after which the position remained steady for a considerable period. Forces reacted to every change in society, adapting and meeting the demand as it arose.

In 1967 there then existed a total of 141 forces in the United Kingdom but a programme of amalgamations had begun, the aim being to enable the resulting larger forces to have the equipment and technical resources to meet the challenge of the future. The result was a reduction to 52 separate forces still locally controlled. Since 1968 police officers have had to react to new policing methods, learn new technological skills, accept new procedural legislation and meet the ever increasing challenge of crime and violence. It can, however, be said that the British police have stood the test of time over the last 160 years and will continue to honour the declaration each makes 'to well and truly serve Her Majesty the Queen in the office of constable without favour or affection, malice or ill will and cause the peace to be kept and preserve and discharge all duties faithfully according to the law'.

PRIMARY POLICE FORCES IN THE UNITED KINGDOM – 1990

ENGLAND

Avon and Somerset Constabulary
Bedfordshire Police
Cambridgeshire Constabulary
Cheshire Constabulary
City of London Police
Cleveland Constabulary
Cumbria Constabulary
Derbyshire Constabulary
Devon & Cornwall Constabulary
Dorset Police
Durham Constabulary
Essex Police
Gloucestershire Constabulary
Greater Manchester Police
Hampshire Constabulary
Hertfordshire Constabulary
Humberside Police
Kent Constabulary
Lancashire Constabulary
Leicestershire Constabulary
Lincolnshire Police
Merseyside Police
Metropolitan Police
Norfolk Constabulary
Northamptonshire Police
Northumbria Police
North Yorkshire Police
Nottinghamshire Constabulary
South Yorkshire Police
Staffordshire Police
Suffolk Constabulary
Surrey Constabulary
Sussex Police
Thames Valley Police
Warwickshire Constabulary
West Mercia Constabulary
West Midlands Police
West Yorkshire Police
Wiltshire Police

WALES

Dyfed-Powys Police
Gwent Constabulary
North Wales Police
South Wales Constabulary

SCOTLAND

Central Scotland Police
Dumfries and Galloway Constabulary
Fife Constabulary
Grampian Police
Lothian and Borders Police
Northern Constabulary
Strathclyde Police
Tayside Police

NORTHERN IRELAND

Royal Ulster Constabulary

UNIFORM AND APPOINTMENTS

A "PEELER", c. 1829

"Peeler" "Robert" or "Bobby" were all early names for a policeman. The latter remains today as an affectionate nickname. The names are a memorial to Sir Robert Peel who was Home Secretary in 1829 and regarded as the creator of the modern police force. Following intense debate, with much opposition, his bill to form the Metropolitan Police was made an Act of Parliament in that year. The Metropolitan Police was born on the 29th September 1829, with a police office established at Scotland Yard.

"PEELER" UNIFORM

The uniform shown is that used by an early policeman and is particularly associated with the "Peeler". It consisted of a navy blue swallow-tailed coat with a raised leather collar — to protect the officer from garrotting, which was rife in London at the time — and blue trousers. In summer, white, lightweight trousers were worn. On the head was the distinctive stovepipe hat. They carried appointments of a truncheon, which was hung from the belt in a leather case, and a rattle for raising the alarm, which was concealed in the pocket of one of the swallow-tails.

THE STOVEPIPE HAT

The need to ensure the police were recognised as a civil body rather than a para-military force was of paramount importance and this was reflected in the style of uniform. The stovepipe hat was based on the civilian beaver top hat, being made of leather and beaver skin over a frame of wire and cane. It was heavy, durable and allegedly strong enough to stand on to gain greater height and visibility. It was used until 1865. The truncheon decorated with the royal crown was the method of signifying a constable's authority.

SENIOR OFFICERS OF THE METROPOLITAN POLICE, 1864

A fine early photograph of Superintendent Robert Walker, on his horse, and Inspectors Baldry, Swanson and Denning at Epsom Races in 1864. They were officers of 'A' Division, Whitehall who attended Epsom for the duration of the races. Superintendent Walker eventually retired in 1886 at the age of 72. Probably one of the last photographs before the demise of the stovepipe hat in 1865.

NORFOLK CONSTABLES, c. 1900

Acts of Parliament of 1835 and 1839 ensured the spread of the police service into every city, borough and later into rural counties. The uniform remained similar to that of the Metropolitan Police. From 1865 the style of uniform changed to the long, closed neck navy blue tunic. The truncheon was moved from the belt to an inside pocket within the trouser leg where it is still kept today. The constables shown have a royal crown and the letter 'N' on the sleeve denoting their force, (Norfolk Constabulary). Two are shown with seniority armbands. All have the helmet replacing the stovepipe hat.

THE BRITISH HELMET

The Edwardian actor William Edouin is wearing the traditional helmet now so distinctive of the British Bobby. Introduced from 1865, the helmet was based on the military helmet of the day. Forces varied the style from the unadorned style, resembling the American Key Stone Cop, to the ornate, with military-style chain and silver spike. Initially they were without helmet plates. These identifying plates developed over a 40-year period based on a sunburst surmounted by a royal crown. In early years the officer's divisional letter and number was included and later the force crest.

SENIOR OFFICERS' UNIFORM, c. 1906

Most forces began with the ranks of Chief Constable, Superintendent and Constable. The rank of Inspector quickly followed and then the lower intermediatory rank of Sergeant. It should be born in mind that no matter what the rank held all are constables within the law. It is generally perceived that the higher the rank the more ornate the uniform. The frock coat was standard for the rank of Superintendent, embelished with ornate trimming, braid and even tassels. The pillar-box type cap was also heavily braided and incorporated the force badge as they became adopted.

"IN FORCE WITH SUNNY JIM"

The advertising card for Sunny Jim and Force cereal, uses the friendly figure of a constable to convey the message. The artist has depicted the truncheon in its leather case on the belt and the bull-nosed lantern. To the side and rear is his rolled cape and the whistle chain is just visible. The cape is unsurpassed in inclement weather whereas the oil-filled lantern with a rotating shield to the light was useful for warming the hands. Whistles replaced the rattle and the battery electric torch replaced the lantern.

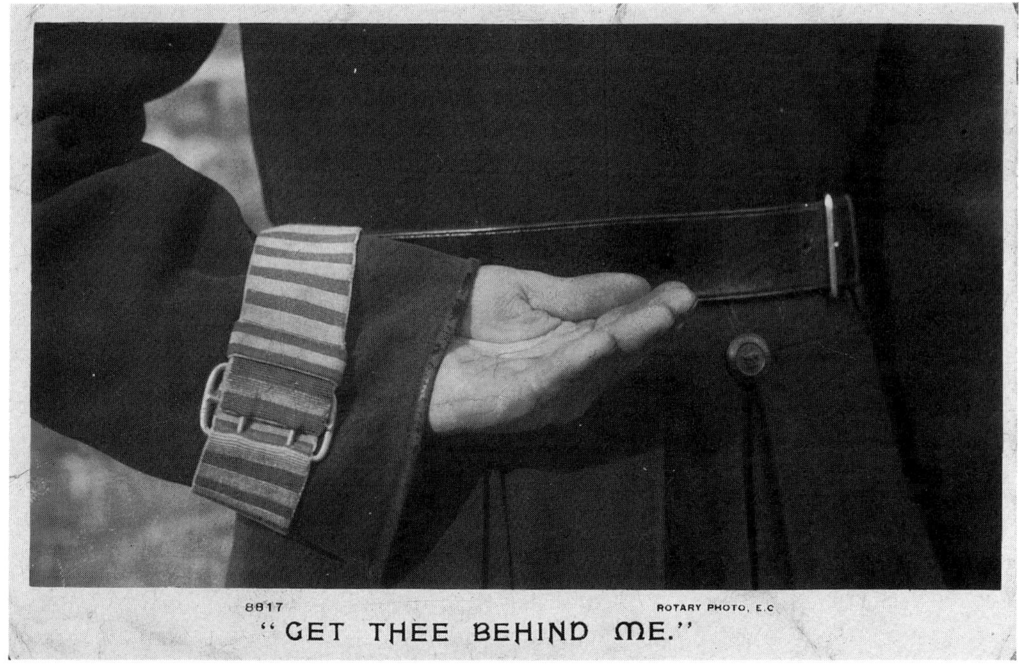

DUTY ARMBANDS

One item not previously mentioned is the armband. The blue and white woven armband, (red and white in the City of London), signified that a policeman was officially on duty. The policeman was always considered to have a twenty-four hour responsibility, however in city and borough forces he travelled to and from duty in uniform, hence the need to distinguish between the two states of duty. The duty armband remained in general use until the period of major amalgamation of Forces in 1968. The armband still remains in the City of London, worn on the left arm by constables and the right arm by sergeants.

TRUNCHEON

The humorous photograph of an American policeman of 1909 shows him brandishing his 'Nut Cracker' or truncheon. The truncheon was used by Parish Constables long before the "Peeler", and remains as standard issue to this day. It is a proud fact that the truncheon is still the only means of available defence to the constable on general patrol today. It is still regarded as a last means of resort and if drawn then it is a subject for report. Contrary to the comment it should never be aimed at the head.

THE WHISTLE

When patrolling it was necessary for a constable to be able to raise an alarm, either as a warning to others or to bring assistance. Originally, this was done by use of a wooden rattle. These were of various design with the favoured one being the compact folding-handle type to fit a pocket. By the late 1880s, the rattle had become unwieldy and inefficient. It was found a whistle would better pierce the increasing noise and bustle of a city. A whistle and chain was then issued to every officer and has been the case to the present day, although some forces are now considering dispensing with the whistle because of the advance of personal radios.

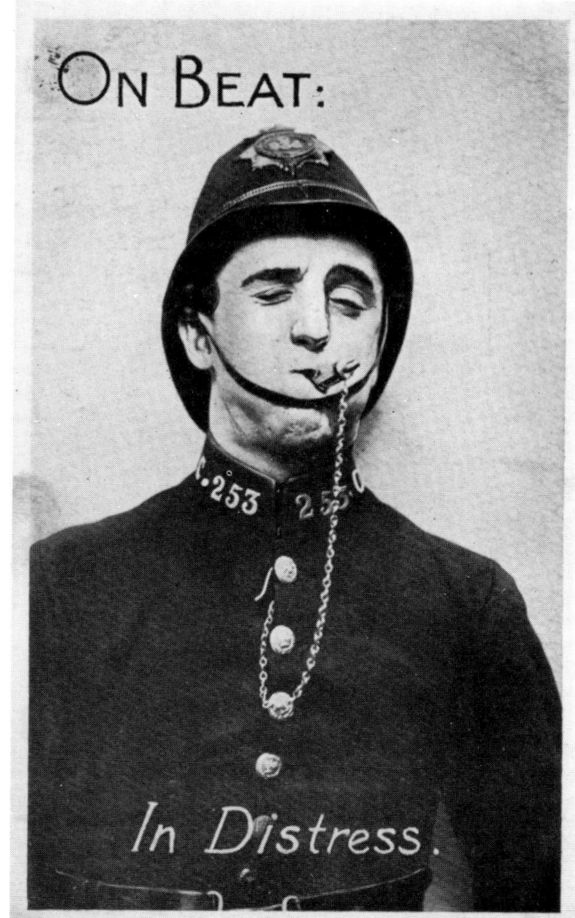

PRODUCING APPOINTMENTS FOR INSPECTION, NORWICH CITY POLICE, c. 1913

Officers reported for duty and paraded the required fifteen minutes before the shift began. They checked correspondence, reports and the latest information, and were then briefed by the Duty Inspector or Sergeant. They would produce appointments for inspection, i.e., truncheon with handcuffs hanging over the end and whistle. The photograph shows the Norwich City Force on parade about 1913 producing such appointments for inspection by an Inspector of Constabulary together with the Chairman of the Watch Committee and the Chief Constable Edwin Winch.

UNIFORM CHANGE, 1949

A significant change in police uniform took effect in 1949 when the open-necked tunic was introduced thereby requiring a shirt collar and necktie which allowed the officer a greater degree of comfort and freedom. Belts and hip pockets have since been dispensed with. Today even greater relaxation can be seen with open-neck shirt sleeve order in the summer, Nato-style pullovers, short car coats and anoraks. A far cry from the restrictive uniform of the "Peeler". The officer is identified as PC Reginald Nicholls of the City of London Police on point duty at Cannon Street/New Change in 1956.

CEREMONIAL DRESS

A Metropolitan Police constable directing traffic in the early 1960s is seen still wearing the closed neck tunic with the Prussian collar. This was due to the fact that a considerable number of state duties had to be performed and the established order of dress for ceremonial duties was still the closed-neck tunic known as "Number ones". These were issued to Metropolitan Officers up to 1971 when the style was finally withdrawn after 74 years of use.

NATO-STYLE HELMETS, 1984

During the 1980s many changes were witnessed in the type of uniform provided for the police. As they became increasingly involved in riots, street crowd disorder and industrial disputes, there was a demand for safer more serviceable uniform whilst in such situations. Fire resistant uniform became standard and the headgear changed from the original helmet to a reinforced one and then to a Nato-style design with visor. These changes, although considered necessary, to some extent altered the image of the policeman by giving a more militaristic look. To redress the balance it should be born in mind that the traditional uniform is still the normal dress of the day. The photograph by Keith Pattison shows policemen wearing Nato-style helmets at Easington, Co. Durham during the mining dispute of 1984.

NEW SCOTLAND YARD, LONDON

The first Metropolitan Police office was a building in Scotland Yard off Whitehall. The photograph shows the second office situated between the Embankment and Whitehall which was known as New Scotland Yard. This was purpose built in 1890 and was designed by the eminent Victorian architect, Richard Norman Shaw. In 1967 the third office was established in Broadway and continues to be known as New Scotland Yard. The Commissioner, Deputy and Assistant Commissioners control the Metropolitan Police Force from the office. These officers, and the Commissioner of the City of London Police were unique in that they were not designated police officers and until recently were ex-officio Justices of the Peace. A reminder of the control J.P.s had over the police prior to 1829.

RURAL POLICEHOUSE, SOUTH MILTON, DEVON, c. 1904

With the formation of rural police forces from 1839, constables were based in a village with each covering a number of parishes. They were given very little instruction or training, being very much left to their own devices. They either had lodgings or lived in small cottages within the village which doubled as the police station. The photograph shows a typical cottage in the village of South Milton, Devon. The central tablet of the sign indicates the divisional letter 'G' and the officer's number '234'. They patrolled on foot and were considered to be always on duty. Theirs was a hard life and often a short one, due to their failing the strict discipline code enforced.

TOWN POLICE STATION, STONE, STAFFORDSHIRE, c. 1908

The growth of the police service on a division, section and beat format required the provision of police stations to house, administer and support the structure. A large building programme was implemented in the late Victorian and Edwardian period. The police station at Stone, Staffs., is a good example usually consisting of accommodation for an inspector and one constable, a public police office and cells. Many had the Petty Sessional Court, known as the Police Court, adjoining and it was serviced by the police. Often Petty Sessional divisions were based on the 'Hundred', the Saxon unit of preventative policing.

BATTERSEA POLICE STATION, LONDON

The Metropolitan Police continued to grow and in 1910 had a total strength of 19,000 officers. The force was divided into 23 Divisions including the Commissioner's Office and the Thames Division, each division being distinguished by letters of the alphabet. The building of police stations had to keep pace with the growth and the photograph shows the officers posing outside the new station at 112–118 Battersea Bridge Road, Battersea in 1912. The card was used by the Daneshill Brick & Tile Works, Basingstoke, as an advertising feature. In the right foreground, notice the fire alarm; part of the street furniture.

MARCHING TO THE BEAT

Having paraded, the beat constables would be marched in line out to their designated beat. On reaching the boundary of the beat, the constable would peel off and the relieved constable would form in line at the rear. On completing the circuit the relieved officers would be dismissed. Every constable had his beat book indicating his route of patrol, reporting points and refreshment break times. Individual collar numbers ensured, as today, that an officer is identifiable whilst on duty in uniform.

"I'M LOST"

This humorous look at a policeman's dilemma on being lost belies the fact that the constable on duty had to be fully conversant with the streets and property on his beat. He was expected to be a fountain of knowledge on all that he surveyed and be able to answer all manner of questions posed by the passers by. One suspects however it was not unknown for directions to have been given in a sure and firm manner, and gratefully received, when in reality the officer was far from confident he had given the correct instructions, particularly when on a new beat.

"I'M LOST."

UNDER POLICE PROTECTION

On the formation of the police the principal functions were the prevention of crime, the detection of offenders, the preservation of the peace and the protection of life and property. However, as society changed additional controls became necessary and these were given to the police. These ranged from the licensing of hackney-carriages, pedlars and chimney sweeps to dealing with lost and found property, animals and the provision of an ambulance and fire service. The officer is shown in a traditional and important role — the help, safety and protection of children.

THE LAST DROP

The greater control of public houses through the Licensing Acts created additional duties for the police in ensuring licensing hours were kept and the drinking laws enforced. It would appear that the early policeman was also partial to a drink and many were fined, reduced in pay or rank or sacked for drinking on duty. The fact that they were considered to be always on duty was ignored. Norfolk Force Orders stated that when out of uniform, an officer could attend a public house but must at all times stand. He was not to accept a drink from anybody else.

SAFETY FIRST

This and the cover photograph are of officers of the City of London Police on duty at the Mansion House. They are escorting pedestrians over the busiest junction in the heart of the City surrounded by the Mansion House, Royal Exchange and Bank. In an endeavour to maintain traffic flow, before the installation of traffic lights, a total of eleven constables were strategically placed on point duty and controlled traffic in a co-ordinated manner. The conjestion by horse-drawn traffic at the turn of the century was as great as any seen since.

A HELPING HAND, c. 1908

Identified as the north-west corner of St. Paul's Churchyard, London, looking towards Paternoster Square. The Constable is proud to be of service in escorting the ageing Bishop into the Cathedral precinct. The iron railings were removed at the time of World War 1, presumably to aid the war effort. The dress of the 'man of the cloth' is as distinctive in its way as that of the constable. Notice the ladies in the height of millinery fashion.

ARREST OF A SUFFRAGETTE, c. 1907

The Womens' Social and Political Union, the Suffragettes, began in 1903 the movement for womens' rights and for the vote. Over the decade they became increasingly militant and directed their wrath against Cabinet ministers and the House of Commons. Their continual demonstrations in Palace Yard brought them into conflict with the police and invited arrest to further their cause. The police constables found them difficult to handle, particularly as there were no female officers to provide a specialist role. They later commenced a bombing campaign and were in open conflict with the police until their cause became forgotten at the outbreak of the First World War.

POLICE AND THE MOTORIST

With the advent of the motor-car, came the eternal conflict between the motorist and the police. As numbers increased and laws were made to control the motorist, then the role of the police materially changed in that hitherto law abiding citizens were being challenged. The need to protect the lives and restrict speeding was the prime requirement. The humorous postcard 'Motoritis' by the artist Charles Crombie, posted in 1916 emphasises the constable's power to arrest for reckless driving. The belief that all policemen had big feet is an important ingredient of the humour.

DEALING WITH A TRAFFIC ACCIDENT

During the two world wars there was a surge in the increase in traffic on the roads with one million vehicles being registered by 1930. As a result traffic accidents became more prevalent and the constable became the arbiter in the issue and recorded the facts. Then, as now, there was a need for adequate insurance. The British Dominion Insurance Company used the postcard to advertise its 'Empire' motor policy which covered all risks and quoted from Shakespeare's 'Othello'. "Wherein I spake of most disastrous changes".

PROTECTION OF PROPERTY, 1925

The movement of money was not such a hazardous task as today, nevertheless the local constable is at hand to escort the slate club money for the annual Christmas payout in 1925.

TO THE RESCUE, NORWICH, 1912

In August, 1912, following a period of torrential rain, the River Wensum flooded large areas of Norwich requiring the emergency services to work to their full capacity. Many were made homeless and a large number of women and children had to be rescued. Police are seen rescuing a child from a cottage upper-floor window. The constable is wearing a summer white straw helmet. He also had to suffer the discomfort of wet feet since modern waterproof rubber boots were not available.

UNDER ATTACK

The duty to quell disorder and violence has always befallen the policeman. At times much of the violence of street brawls is a form of aggravated amusement for the participants which turns into a co-ordinated attack on the police officer directed to deal with the incident. The card published by Valentine of Dundee encapsulates such an attitude — one participant advising the other "Go and find a peeler for yourself".

TAKEN INTO CUSTODY

A Raphael Tuck 'Real Photograph' postcard, series 3715, shows a London street scene in the early 1930s. Some hilarity is expressed as the sergeant observes the constable taking a stray dog into custody. One of the extraneous duties placed upon the police was the task of registering and housing lost and found dogs.

THE BENEVOLENT POLICEMAN

Another Raphael Tuck postcard from the same series, highlighting the role and concern of P.C. 366 of the Holborn Division of the Metropolitan Police to ensure the young lad safely across the street. The white arm sleeves were strapped to the arm whilst performing point duty. The card, posted in 1936, states: "To pilot children over crowded roads is daily proof of the policeman's kind and efficient service."

THE BENEVOLENT POLICEMAN

CEREMONIAL DUTIES, BRECON, c. 1930

The police have always been part of the pomp and pageantry of the ceremonial occasion. This extends to royal visits, mayor making or the opening of the County Assizes or today's counterpart, the Crown Court. Officers of the Breconshire Constabulary are escorting the Judge from his lodgings at The Struet, Brecon to the Assize Court. The police officers are carrying long tipped staves and the buglers are soldiers from the Military Barracks at Brecon. The Breconshire Constabulary with 66 officers amalgamated in 1948 with the Mid-Wales Police. Today it is part of the Dyfed-Powys Police.

STATE OCCASION – THE FUNERAL OF KING EDWARD VII, 1910

The controlling of crowds has always been a prime duty of the police and as such large numbers of men are required to either line the route or to marshall the crowd. Such control is always dependent upon the good humour or reverence of the mass of people and is obviously influenced by the occasion. Recent events have seen disruptive elements at work in the crowd requiring a change in police strategy in that now the police officers invariably face the crowd. King Edward VII laid in state in Westminster Hall for three days from the 17 May, 1910 during which time many thousands of people filed past to pay their respects.

28 FUNERAL PROCESSION OF HIS LATE MAJESTY KING EDWARD VII. — Edinburgh Police. — LL.

EDINBURGH POLICE ON PARADE, 1910

Following the death of King Edward VII on the 6th May, 1910, the political constitutional crisis that was in being at the time, was suspended during the period of mourning. On the 20th May, large crowds lined the streets of London, to witness the State funeral procession of the late King from Westminster Hall to Paddington. The police service was represented by a number of Forces, one of which was the Edinburgh Police with a contingent of 26 officers and men.

AWAITING ROYAL DUTY, 1907

There is little doubt that all leave would have been cancelled for the City of London officers waiting in King Street to take up their position for a royal occasion. The streets are garlanded for the visit of the Kaiser Wilhelm II and the Kaiserin who processed to the Guildhall for a state occasion on the 13th November, 1907. The weather was kind allowing open carriages to be used to the delight of the large crowds lining the route under the watchful eyes of the constables.

SPECIAL RESERVE, METROPOLITAN POLICE, c. 1908

In many ways the police structure followed that of the military, and the sergeant rank is no exception. In the majority of forces, sergeants were appointed at the beginning, in others they followed later. In London mature first-class sergeants and constables were selected as a reserve contingent to attend at state and special occasions. They were granted extra pay and were identified by the additional letter 'R' on the collar. Such a contingent are seen parading with an army warrant officer. The reserve was disbanded in 1913. The four stripes, later three surmounted by a crown, indicated a station sergeant, which evolved from within the sergeant rank and was held by those with long service and the status of supervising the Police Station.

POLICE HORSE "PRETENDER" IN THE MALL, LONDON, 1939

The horse became an important aid to policing. As the volume of horse-drawn vehicles increased and reached its peak in the Edwardian period, there was a need for the police to be equally mobile. The horse gave height and added authority to the mounted officer and was of enormous benefit when participating in public order events. The long truncheon was standard issue and available for use should crowd disorder dictate. In these modern times horses are used for crowd control, street patrol and ceremonial duties continue with the provision of escorts to royal events, state visits and mayoral coaches.

RURAL CONSTABLE ON HORSE PATROL, c. 1907

The use of the horse for patrol work in rural parishes was a welcome innovation and provided an affinity with the local population who also relied heavily on the mobility afforded by the horse. Most police forces had their own mounted branch at some stage in their history, mostly during the period from 1900 to 1918. Today mounted branches are to be found in twelve forces, invariably those with large conurbations of population. The riders and horses are always in demand to show off their skills of horsemanship at major shows and gymkhanas.

MOUNTED BRANCH, NORWICH CITY POLICE, c. 1912

The sixteen horses of the Norwich City Police are groomed and alert ready for inspection. The senior officer on parade is of Superintendent rank and deputy to the Chief Constable. Not only were the horses used for police duty, they were also used by the police/fire brigade to pull the fire engine. Originally, horses were hired as and when needed to pull the fire engine. In 1903, following problems of supply, the Watch Committee purchased four horses for the purpose. They were also used for police patrol and the conveyance of prisoners. One was for the Chief Constable's personal use. As the number of fire engines increased so did the horses.

THAMES POLICE, c. 1890

Theft in the Port of London reached such enormous proportions that in 1790 the West India Merchants adopted a plan by Dr. Patrick Colquhoun for policing the River Thames. The first Marine Office was opened at Wapping on the site of the present Divisional Headquarters of the Thames Police. The marine police were successful in restricting crime on the river, patrolling from Battersea to Woolwich. In 1839 the Marine Police were amalgamated into the Metropolitan Police and in 1885 moved from rowing galleys and sail to steam-driven launches. One steam-launch being the *Chowkidar* (Nightwatchman) seen at the police station at Waterloo Pier about 1890. Today modern fully equipped craft patrol the 54 miles of the Thames from Staines Bridge to Dartford Creek.

RIVER POLICE, GRIMSBY, c. 1911

The rivers were the arteries of trade being far more accessible than the turnpike road network. Forces with a thriving port had a police presence on the water to prevent smuggling and the pilfering of cargo. Rowing boats such as the one at Grimsby were often used at night with muffled oars to help conceal their presence. The back of the card states 'A man severe he was and stern to view. This is how the policeman does his beat here.'

DETECTIVE OFFICERS, METROPOLITAN POLICE, c. 1920

Senior detectives Superintendents Hawkins and Wensley and Acting Superintendents Carlin and Neil, were known as the Big Four of New Scotland Yard in 1919. The force was divided into four detective areas each controlled by one of the superintendents. It was also common practice, up to 1968, for Metropolitan detectives to attend other forces to assist in investigating major crimes and murders. A Detective Department was first formed in 1842 with the prime aim of investigating crime, the officers working in plain clothes. They worked from the Commissioners' Office and were viewed with suspicion. By 1868 there were only 15 detectives in a force of nearly 8,000. Gradually professional expertise was acquired and in 1878 the department was reorganised and was called the Criminal Investigation Department.

POLICE DOGS, 1938

The first police dogs to join a force were the black labradors "Nigger" and "Smut". They are seen being introduced to their handlers at Peckham, London on the 12th May, 1938. The war held up their general introduction after which dogs were introduced in all forces, being mainly German Shepherd dogs, to assist in the pursuit and tracking of criminals. Dogs have in recent years been trained to find drugs and explosives by utilizing their sensitivity to smell. The exploits and gallantry of countless police dogs will be ever remembered and records fifty years of proud service.

APPREHENDED, c. 1905

A humorous card by Dudley Hardy and published by Davidson Brothers highlights one of the more dispicable actions, that of hoax fire, accident or bomb calls. Inevitably a swift response is made thereby putting the emergency services, and to some extent the people on the streets, at risk.

NORWICH CITY POLICE FIRE BRIGADE IN ACTION, 1913

The Municipal Reform Act 1835 allowed cities and boroughs to provide a fire service. Norwich in keeping with most cities did so and having just appointed a police force linked the two services. A number of police officers were also designated firemen and received additional remuneration but had to live in a section house and be on call when off police duty. The Chief Fire Officer was the Chief Constable and the brigade was controlled by the Watch Committee. This situation applied until 1941, during the Second World War, when the National Fire Service was formed. The Brigade are seen returning from a fire at Hellesdon Mill on 4th May, 1913.

NORWICH POLICE FIRE BRIGADE, MERRYWEATHER ENGINE, c. 1911

The first motorised vehicle was a Merryweather fire-engine purchased in 1911 for £948. This was used in tandem with the horse-drawn steam engines but enabled the brigade to cut travelling time in attending fires and thereby assist in saving life and property. The Norwich police fire-brigade was also extending cover to outlying parishes for which they levied a standing charge. By 1939 the whole force of 144 officers doubled as firemen, together with a number of part-time Auxilliary Fire Service volunteers. A few officers transferred to the new National Fire Service in 1941 but most were pleased to concentrate on policing duties.

FIRST AID TRAINING

By the very nature of his duties a police officer has always had the need to be proficient in first aid. From the beginning of formalised training, the teaching of first aid has been part of the curriculum based on the St. John's Ambulance syllabus. It was the practice in many forces for every officer to wear a St. John's Ambulance medallion on the sleeve of his tunic. Annual competitions were held both within forces and nationally against other organisations, notably the railway and major companies in industry. Norfolk officers are seen being tested under competition rules in 1967.

AID TO THE INJURED, c. 1906

Metropolitan officers of the Whitehall Division are seen conveying a casualty through the streets of London. They are using a police-operated wheeled-litter to transport a patient to the nearest hospital. Wheeled-litters were housed at police stations throughout the capital and were available for call out when required. Following the advent of motorised ambulances the litters were still retained for back-up use.

CITY OF LONDON POLICE AMBULANCE, 1907

In 1907 the City of London Police Committee established a mobile ambulance system with a linked network of communication via 52 white police pillars strategically placed throughout the city. A call from a pillar to a central control ensured the dispatch of one of three Electromobile ambulances to the scene. They were manned by a trained driver and police officer who gave first aid at the scene and conveyed the injured to one of the city hospitals. The City Police operated the ambulance service until 1949.

VEHICLES ON PARADE, c. 1930

In keeping with most cities, Norwich Watch Committee commissioned an ambulance service and designated it a police function. Officers were assigned ambulance duties and the system was controlled from the police station. By 1930 three wooden-bodied ambulances were in use and were called on 1793 occasions to give assistance. This service continued throughout the Second World War until ultimately the responsibility was handed over to the National Health Committee on the 5th July, 1948.

WOMEN POLICE, SWANSEA, 1918

The need for women police was established during World War I as women became more liberated whilst working in munitions, other industries, transport and on the land. There were also camp followers to contend with. All in their way required a police commitment, often being one of guidance and understanding. The women's movement formed the Women Police Volunteers who were given permission to perform duty at main line railway stations. They also enforced curfews on women which created conflict in the movement, upon which, a Miss Dawson broke away and formed the 'Womens Police Service' to which these ladies from Swansea belonged.

The Converted Suffragette !

POLICEWOMEN IN WAR TIME

Chief Officers were pleased to utilize the skills of the women volunteer officers but were reluctant to see them as fully fledged members of a police force. They would not issue a warrant card but gave a written authority for them to call on the services of a police officer as required. The Metropolitan Police in 1914 approached the National Union of Woman Workers to provide women patrols in the capital to work with women and girls. Within six months the organisation had been formed with over 500 volunteer patrols. Eventually there was confusion and difficulty in differentiating between the two bodies then in being. In 1920 the Metropolitan Commissioner prosecuted the Women's Police Service Volunteers after which they became the Women's Auxiliary Service, leaving the way clear for one group to develop the role in the capital.

A FAIR COP

It was the Sex Disqualification (Removal) Act of 1919 that finally dispelled any legal doubts on a policewoman's status. Although there was still opposition to the concept of women police, their expertise in dealing with women and children was recognised and the Home Office began to encourage their recruitment and ultimately they were employed throughout the country. From 1923 they gradually became attested and full members of the police service. Today women officers are an increasing percentage of every police force and have equal standing with their male colleagues. The Art and Humorous Publishing Company's card by Fred Spurgin highlights one of their roles in dealing with children.

WOMAN OFFICER ON THE BEAT, 1986

W.P.C. Sheila Edwards of the Hampshire Constabulary patrolling her beat by cycle at Basingstoke in 1986. Wearing her bowler police hat and Nato-style pullover, she epitomises the modern police woman. With a personal radio on an ultra high frequency, she would have been in contact with her local police station at all times, giving her the support of all police resources from additional back-up to the information stored in the Police National Computer. Hampshire, in common with all forces, are endeavouring to increase the presence of police officers on the beat.

SPECIAL CONSTABLE OBTAINING PROFESSIONAL ADVICE

The role of the special constable to assist the police in an emergency has been a long and honourable one. As the policing of this country is invested in all citizens, it has always been the case that those charged with the responsibility could appoint 'specials' as required. The first Act of Parliament was passed in 1673, again at the time of the Modern Police in 1831, and today the authority for their being is in the Police Act 1964. In the early years their main value was as a large body of men readily available to help quell crowd disorder and maintain the peace. Gradually, they have been trained in basic police duties to enable them to be effective in the event of an emergency.

SPECIAL POLICE INSPECTOR P. ROGERS, CARDIFF CITY POLICE

As World War I depleted the number of regular officers, the majority of forces enrolled significant numbers of special constables. They were not normally uniformed, being issued with a cap, badge, whistle, armband, truncheon and warrant card. In this case the leather shoulder strap and badge is probably an indication of rank. They received no remuneration for their labours being true volunteers with a sense of service to the community. This situation remains today although a 'special' wears a uniform and is reimbursed any expenses.

SPECIAL CONSTABULARY ARMBAND

Those special constables appointed in World War I were organised under their own command structure but all were required to respond and assist the instruction given by a regular officer of any rank. They were recruited from all walks of life but a large number came from the business community. The humorous card by Fred Spurgin clearly shows their mark of office, the khaki armband with the King George crown in red.

CITY OF LONDON SPECIAL CONSTABULARY, 1911

The year 1911 was one of industrial unrest throughout the country with dockers, miners, railwaymen and other workers involved in disputes to varying degrees of intensity and violence. This stretched the resources of the regular police resulting in the use of special constables to assist in policing the disputes. The 'specials' were assigned static and patrol duties at strategic points affected by the strikes. The photograph shows the Lord Mayor of London inspecting City of London special constables after completing duty in connection with the Railway strike.

MEDAL PRESENTATION, 1919

The photograph shows Commander Bullock of the Metropolitan Police presenting the Special Constabulary Long Service Medal to a 'special' with the rank of chief inspector. King George V instituted the medal to mark the service rendered by special constables during the Great War 1914–18. Police medals for regular officers include the Queens Police Medal for distinguished service originally instituted as the King's Police Medal 1909 by King Edward VII, the Police Long Service and Good Conduct Medal instituted in 1951 by King George VI and awarded after 22 years meritorious service and Coronation and Jubilee medals. A number of distinguished officers receive awards in the Queen's New Year and Birthday Honours lists.

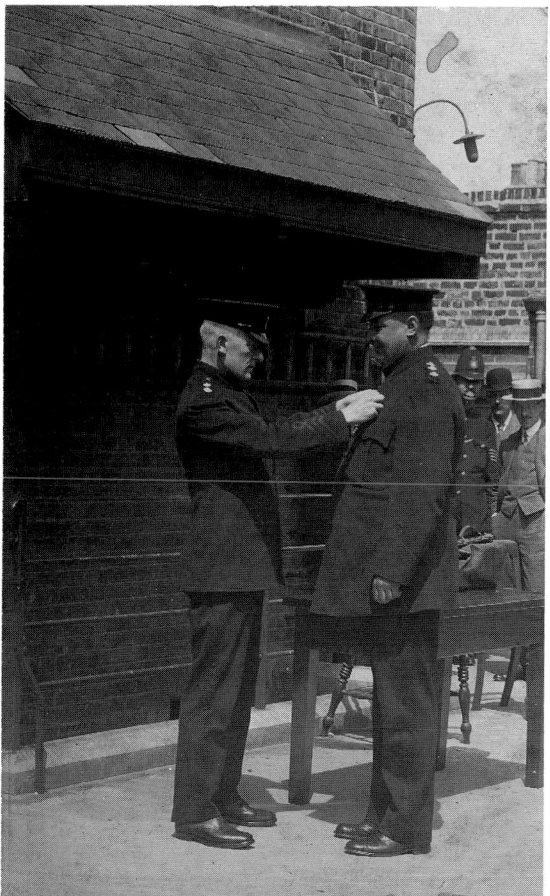

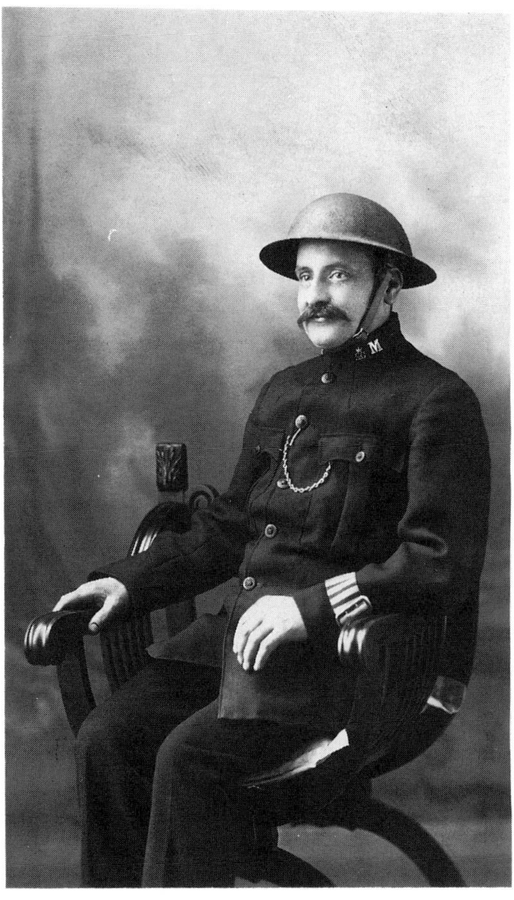

SPECIAL CONSTABLE, c. 1942

The need for special constables during the Second World War was as great as in the First World War. At the beginning of hostilities in 1939, thousands of police officers joined the colours thereby depleting forces of considerable patrol strength. Many retired police officers returned as War Reserves and thousands of citizens volunteered to join the Special Constabulary to be trained in wartime policing. They were issued with a uniform similar to the regular force but with a cap rather than a helmet. They were also issued with a tin helmet of which the wearer is obviously very proud.

CHIEF CONSTABLE OF KING'S LYNN, 1915

The Chief Constable of the King's Lynn Borough Force, Charles William Hunt is seen in his best frock-coated uniform breaking what is now a cardinal rule, in that he is shown handling an unexploded bomb. The bomb was dropped in an air raid on 19th January, 1915. In the early evening the same day, a German Zeppelin airship travelled over the Norfolk coast dropping the very first bombs on England against the small coastal towns, including Gt. Yarmouth, Sheringham, Snettisham and King's Lynn.

AIR RAID WARNING — TAKE COVER, c. 1915

The German Zeppelins increased their range and began bombing London. One of the additional wartime duties of the police was to give warning of an air raid. The photograph shows constables of the Greenwich Division of the Metropolitan Police ready to leap on their cycles to patrol the streets raising the alarm by blowing their whistles and advising the public to take cover. The placards were worn front and back for maximum effect!

TAKE COVER, 1918

This humorous postcard postally used in 1918 reflects the image of the portly, friendly constable offering protection to young children. The artist has used the 'Air raid — Take Cover' notice to make the point. As, prior to the war, the majority of postcards had been printed in Germany, the card proudly states it is of British manufacture.

POLICE IN NOTTINGHAMSHIRE, 1893

From the early formation of police forces, it has been the practice to provide mutual aid to other forces in times of emergency or major disputes. During a mining dispute and colliery riots in Nottinghamshire in 1893 a request was made for such assistance. Several forces, including Norfolk, provided police officers to help quell the riots and maintain the peace. The photograph shows five Norfolk officers with the host sergeant from Nottinghamshire. The variation in uniform is particularly noticeable.

SOHO STREET, LIVERPOOL, TRADE DISPUTE AND STRIKE, 1911

The workers unrest in 1911 was throughout the country and was particularly strong in Liverpool. It began in the docks in January when the scalers and cementers went on strike. The disturbance reached its peak in August when the transport workers demonstrated on St. George's Hall Plateau. The crowd was in a militant mood and following an arrest by the police the crowd retaliated with violent attacks on the police, throwing stones, bottles, iron bolts and using wooden staves or truncheons taken from injured policemen. Running battles followed through the side streets in the Islington area.

PRISON VANS, LIVERPOOL STRIKE, 1911

The mounted police were called to clear Lime Street and the Riot Act was read. As well as the Birmingham Police who had been drafted to Liverpool, the Warwickshire Regiment was used to assist the local police under the control of Assistant Head Constable Mr. F. Caldwell. Over 200 rioters and police were injured and Lime Street Station and St. George's Hall were used as casualty clearing stations. Problems continued through the month with shortages of food and no electricity, even the pubs closed early. Over 4000 special constables were enrolled. The movement of prisoners to Walton Gaol required an escort of the Royal Scots Greys.

S.S.AARO, HULL STRIKE, 1911

A large contingent of Yorkshire policemen are seen on board the Steamship *Aaro* in Hull Dock on 14th June, 1911. They are well prepared with haversack rations and water bottles. The Hull seamen were fully involved in the labour dispute and strike with 4,000 meeting in Paragon Square, Hull on 14th June. A rocket was to be fired signifying the strike action. On or about the 21st June, a one-day token strike was called at the Wilson Steamship Company, owner of the *S.S. Aaro,* when only 40 of the 800 workers reported for work.

BOROUGH & COUNTY POLICE, MANCHESTER, LABOUR DISPUTE, 1911

The massed ranks of the Manchester Borough Police together with their County colleagues from neighbouring forces show the numbers of men needed to police the labour dispute of 1911 in Manchester. Police matrons are also in evidence. As elsewhere, Manchester's main problems were in the month of August when they assumed a grave phase with all the railway workers on strike supporting their fellow workers in Liverpool and refusing to handle goods from that city. Troops were used to guard all the main railway establishments. The workers were vehemently against Lloyd George's conciliation scheme believing it bound them in chains.

THE CREW OF R.M.S. OLYMPIC UNDER ARREST, 25TH April 1912

Following the sinking of the *Titanic,* there was concern from the crew of the White Star Line sister-ship *Olympic* as to their safety. Prior to sailing, the firemen stokers were not satisfied with the number of lifeboats provided, although a further 24 had been fitted. The firemen went on strike against union advice and walked off with their kit at Southampton. Seventeen firemen had remained on board and others were recruited but when the seamen showed sympathy for a demand to sack those seventeen the voyage was cancelled. On the 25th April, 1912, fifty-three men were arrested for wilfully disobeying the command of the captain and conveyed to Portsmouth. They were handed into the custody of the Borough Police and marched to the Town Hall under a strong escort. It was stated that the firemen appeared in the best of spirits spending time smoking and singing.

METROPOLITAN POLICE 'L' DIVISION IN SOUTH WALES, 1910

Political unrest and draconian measures taken by the Liberal Party resulted in a degree of class warfare and claim for recognition by the Trade Unions during 1910 and 1911. In South Wales the coal miners took disruptive action on a wide scale resulting in the local forces requesting police support from around the country. A group of 'L' Division officers of the Metropolitan Police were at Tonypandy on the 27th November, 1910 and are seen in a relaxed manner with the locals at the pit.

CHRISTMAS CHEER, PONTYPRIDD, 1910

The South Wales mining dispute continued throughout the winter requiring the Metropolitan Police officers to maintain support to keep the peace. It is a fact that away from the glare of publicity, whether in 1910 or 1984, the miners and policemen developed a good humoured rapport and understanding thereby keeping confrontation to a minimum. It was not unusual for sporting events to take place between the two bodies. Feeding the inner man was important and to this end the traditional Christmas lunch was provided and appreciated at Pontypridd.

BRIGHTON BOROUGH POLICE, 1926

In 1926 during the General Strike, the Brighton Borough Police Force sent a contingent of officers to South Wales. They are seen parading outside the Police Station in East Street, Brighton on their return. Of those with medals, in the centre wearing the Military Cross is PC 207 Wood. The floral tribute declares 'A duty well done' and incorporates the police helmet and armband. It is noticeable that the moustache had become less fashionable by 1926. Posters can be seen offering substantial rewards for the recovery of lost property.

MINING DISPUTE, EASINGTON, CO. DURHAM, 1984

In 1984, as in 1893, 1911 and 1926 the police were once again required to be involved in a mining dispute. The police, often to their own concern and that of sections of the community were required to stand between miners and enforce legislation on picketing and the right to work. Bitter confrontation became inevitable with the majority of the mining community believing that the police were enforcing government policy rather than acting as a neutral independent body. During the year-long dispute there were many issues of conflict yet on other occasions sensitive policing and good humour between both parties prevailed. The photograph by Keith Pattison encapsulates the mood at the entrance to the Easington Colliery, Co., Durham on the 24th August, 1984.

POLICE STRIKE, 1919

From its inception the police service had subjected its members to severe restrictions on domestic life, long hours and harsh arbitarily imposed conditions of service. Once the First World War was over the underlying deep seated resentment surfaced and protest followed. Policemen throughout the country protested, and in London many marches and demonstrations took place and 6,000 took strike action. The photograph shows the Lambeth Branch of the National Union of Police & Prison Officers marching through South London declaring that 'Tyranny is not discipline' and 'Let the punishment fit the crime'. The strike was not total yet the feeling was such that the Home Secretary instructed that Lord Desborough should chair a committee to consider police conditions of service and make recommendations. A large proportion of the striking policemen were sacked thereby leaving those in service to benefit from their action.

WALLINGTON BRANCH'S BELIEF THAT 'UNITY IS STRENGTH'

Wallington Branch's banner representing twelve London police stations and believing that 'Unity is Strength' is followed by the British Railway Police contingent. Some immediate improvements were made, but two localised token strikes materialised in 1919 before faith was restored. Within a year Desborough had reported and the Police Act 1919 was passed. The conditions of service were improved and more importantly many of the recommendations were made law in Police Regulations. The regulations allowed for policemen to be represented by a body known as The Police Federation, drawn from the ranks of the service from chief inspector and below to promote activities relating to the welfare of its members and the efficiency of the service. The Police Federation, together with the Police Superintendents' Association and the Association of Chief Police Officers still effect the same role today. Since 1919 the police officer has been barred from a trade union and has no right to strike action.

FUNERAL PROCESSION OF P.C. ALGER, GREAT YARMOUTH BOROUGH POLICE, August 1909

As today, a police officer never knows what awaits him in the course of his duty. On the 18th August, 1909, Police Constable 37 Charles Alger was sent to deal with a complaint received that a man was beating his wife. On attending he found the man, Thomas Allen, in his garden and on being approached the man produced a shortened double-barrelled breach-loading gun. He fired at the constable, killing him with wounds to the face and neck. He was arrested, found guilty and sentenced to be hanged. He was later reprieved on the grounds of insanity and committed to Broadmoor. P.C. Alger, who was 37 years of age, was buried with full police honours at Gorleston, the whole force parading and processing from the church to the cemetery.

FUNERAL OF P.C. TYLER, 29th JANUARY, 1909

P.C. 403 Tyler paid the ultimate price having been shot and killed on the 23rd January, 1909, in pursuit of two Latvian anarchists through the streets of Tottenham. This followed a robbery when shots were fired resulting in a two-hour chase in which there were 25 casualties, two of them fatal, P.C. Tyler and a ten-year-old boy Ralph Joselyne. The two anarchists finally shot themselves rather than be caught. P.C. Tyler was given a public funeral during which large crowds paid homage. Among the wreaths was one from the Imperial Russian Consul-General.

HOUNDSDITCH MURDERS, 16th December, 1910

This card was published in memory of three brave policemen who were brutally murdered by Bolshevik revolutionaries in Houndsditch, City of London. Sergeant Bentley, Constable Choat and Sergeant Tucker were shot at close range whilst tackling the gang and two other officers, Sergeant Bryant and Constable Woodhouse were shot and crippled for life. The Latvian gang had intended to rob a jeweller's shop to obtain Tsarist wealth to fund the revolution in Russia. The events that followed became known as the Sidney Street Siege. In the New Year Honours of 1911 the King awarded the King's Police Medal to the three officers, presenting the medals to their nearest relative. (The name of Constable Choat is incorrectly spelt on the card).

THE BATTLE OF SIDNEY STREET, STEPNEY

Following the Houndsditch murders, two of the Latvian gang were known to be in a house in Sidney Street. On the 2nd January, 1911, the house was surrounded by armed police with shotguns. The Latvians commenced firing and the siege began. Winston Churchill as Home Secretary attended and authorised the use of the Scots Guards with their rifles. In the shooting that followed one Latvian was killed and the other, rather than surrender when the house caught fire, suffocated to death. In all the siege lasted eight hours. The connected murders and siege required the two London forces to work together to resolve the issue.

METROPOLITAN POLICE MEMORIAL SERVICE, 1919

Following the cessation of hostilities and the 'peace' declared in 1918, the country counted the cost of the conflict in lives lost. In keeping with all parts of the community, the police service mourned the loss of many former officers who had served their country by giving their lives. In 1919 peace marches and processions were held throughout the country. The Metropolitan Police held their own memorial service in Westminster Abbey on the 17th May, 1919. The officers representing the Force can be seen parading from the direction of Parliament Square.

POPPY DAY, CASTLE ACRE, NORFOLK, c. 1925

Constables Runacres, Beaumont and Balls are seen ready for parade on a damp November day in 1925. The two ladies are selling poppies for the Earl Haig's Remembrance Day Appeal. The British Legion sold the first poppies in 1921 and opened a small factory in 1922 employing disabled servicemen. Today about 45 million poppies are made, raising in excess of £10 million. The police service has always participated in Remembrance Day parades and officers still wear the poppy on their uniform with pride.

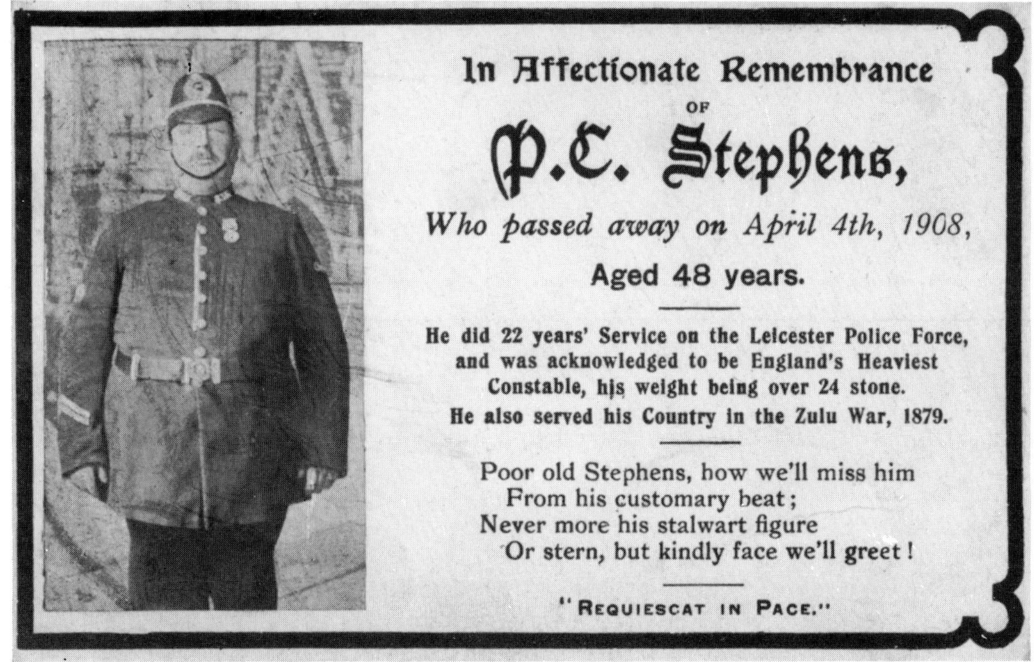

P.C. STEPHENS, LEICESTER POLICE

Occasionally a constable becomes famous in his own right. One such man was P.C. Stephens of the Leicester Police. Performing his duties in the main Granby Street and Clock Tower area he was known to all with affection and for his size. At 23 stone, being England's heaviest policeman, his death from natural causes on 4th April, 1908 was mourned by all Leicester with thousands lining the streets for his funeral procession on the 8th April. His esteem was such that a number of remembrance postcards were produced and sent with such comments as 'Sorry this gentleman has left us'. Truly a great man in all respects.

CYCLES ON PARADE, NORWICH, c. 1912

For the policeman restricted to being on foot with often fifteen or more parishes to cover in rural areas, the advent of the bicycle must have heralded a significant move forward in ease of transportation. The photograph shows a contingent of the Norwich City Police on parade with their high-framed police model cycles. Forces were, however, reluctant at the turn of the century to expend money on such purchases. Some sanctioned the hire of cycles, in an emergency, to be ridden at the rider's risk. In time it became the accepted mode of transport for rural officers.

SUPERVISORY PATROL BY HORSE AND TRAP, c. 1920

This fine horse and trap is of the type provided for Superintendents to patrol their large rural divisions for the purpose of supervision, attendance at Courts and to be present at operational meetings. Superintendent W. Roy of the East Dereham Division of the Norfolk Constabulary is ready for the journey but subject to the Force Order not to exceed six miles per hour.

PONTARDAWE DIVISION, GLAMORGAN, c. 1905

A fine group of Pontardawe policemen leaving their division for a destination unknown, possibly for duty at a major event or to a centralised Force parade. Note the Welsh style of uniform with the peaked cap. Two are shown to be carrying a hanger, a curved sword similar to a cutlass, of the type issued to selected constables. Without exception they are moustached as were practically all policemen of the era. The Franson char-à-banc was made by the Commercial Motor Company, Luton, being solid-tyred, chain-driven and with a curtained canopy for inclement weather.

WILTSHIRE CONSTABULARY ON THE MOVE, c. 1920

Nineteen members of the Wiltshire Constabulary in a relaxed mood whilst waiting for Mr. A. Strode's char-à-banc from Swindon to commence its journey. Photographed by Whitworth of Salisbury, it is likely the policemen had been moved down to Salisbury from north of the Force area. It would appear the vehicle was hired with a driver, shown in the white coat, but the inspector was allowed to preserve status by sitting behind the wheel.

POLICE MOTOR-CYCLE PATROL c. 1930

Prior to 1914 very few forces had any form of motorised transport. From 1919 forces found it necessary to purchase vehicles for patrol duty, transport of personnel and for speed of operation. Initially the motor-cycle was the cheapest and easiest method of patrol and was widely used. Shown ready for inspection at Norwich about 1930 is a B.S.A. three-wheeler, two B.S.A. motor-cycle combinations, and two solo motor-cycles, one being a Triumph. Motor-cars were also introduced and used by Chief Officers and for special duties.

TALBOT PATROL CARS, c. 1939

The seven Talbot two-seater touring cars were introduced in Norfolk in 1939 for use on general police duties and mobile patrol and stationed throughout the county. As forces increased their traffic fleets they began to create separate traffic departments specialising in all aspects of road traffic law and duties. The drivers were given advanced training and expected to set an example on the road. Today forces have technically sophisticated vehicles in their specialist branches to meet the ultimate challenge on the roads and motorways and numerous general purpose vehicles for basic patrol and supervisionary work.

VELOCETTE ON THE BEAT

In the early 1960s the life on the beat for the policeman was made easier by providing increased mobility. The water-cooled Velocette model LE was introduced and is being used by the author at Nelson's birthplace, Burnham Thorpe, Norfolk in 1963. The versatility of the machine allowed quiet but rapid coverage of the beat and at the same time its ease of use enabled contact to be maintained with the members of the community. It was known as the 'Noddy Bike' due to the similarity with the bike used by Noddy in Enid Blyton's popular childrens' books.

HILLMAN IMP PANDA CARS, 1968

Panda cars, so called because of their striped livery, became part of the policing scene in every major city and town in 1968. They were part of the Unit Beat System. The car being manned and patrolling the area of a number of foot beats 24 hours a day. The foot beats were patrolled by a regular constable eight hours a day, on varying shift patterns, with the aim for him to get to know his community. In addition the use of pocket radios became widespread allowing officers increased contact with the police station and more efficient response in attending incidents.

Waiting for the Tulip Parade, Spalding 394M

MODERN MOTOR-CYCLE, c. 1986

The modern police motor-cyclist is well equipped for the task. The latest machines and protective clothing provide the officer with the means of maintaining a fast but safe response to incidents on our conjested roads. Their versatility allows for many and varied duties, including escorts for royal visits, judges or the ponderous movement of a wide load. The officers of the Lincolnshire Force with a BMW R80 machine are enjoying a more tranquil duty in leading the annual Spalding Tulip Parade.

PEEL HOUSE, S.W.1.

PEEL HOUSE TRAINING SCHOOL

The earlier Peel House in central London was the training school for thousands of Metropolitan police officers. Today it is established at the Peel Centre, Hendon. The other 42 forces of England and Wales have recruits trained at one of six District Training Centres based in differing parts of the country. In addition officers receive continuation training within their own Force Training Establishments. Knowledge of the law and police duties are the constables' tools of trade.

POLICE STAFF COLLEGE, RYTON-ON-DUNSMORE, c. 1953

In 1947 recommendations were made that a Police College should be established for the higher training of the future leaders of the police service and for the organisation of training courses for higher ranks. The Home Office approved the recommendations and in 1948, a National Police College was inaugurated in temporary accommodation at Ryton-on-Dunsmore, Warwickshire. A permanent home for the College was then made at Bramshill House, Nr. Hartney Wintney, Hampshire, a fine Jacobean mansion set in 270 acres of parkland. The transfer was made in 1960 where the college remains to this day.

POLICE CONVALESCENT HOME, HOVE, SUSSEX

The rigours of police duty and the aftermath of violence dictated the need for police convalescent homes for officers to attend and recuperate. To this end the Police Seaside Home at Hove was established in 1890 and the St. Andrew's Convalescent Home at Harrogate in 1898 by Miss Catherine Gurney, O.B.E., for the benefit of the police of all ranks of the Southern and Northern Forces respectively. Their requirement is as great today, however, the Southern Home is now established at Flint House, Goring on Thames.

RESIDENTS AT THE POLICE SEASIDE HOME, HOVE, 1909

A group of moustached residents at the home in April 1909 are well on the way to recovery. The card was probably sent by one of the officers in the Bath chairs as he states in May that he had dispensed with his old friend and was back in full business again. Today not only do the homes offer excellent accommodation in pleasant surroundings, but provide a full range of orthopædic and therapeutic facilities to aid in the recovery from injuries of violence.

METROPOLITAN AND CITY ORPHANAGE, TWICKENHAM

In the 1870s police families suffered, as others, through the period of large families, poverty and disease, resulting in premature death. There was little welfare or assistance available. Accepting the need, the Orphanage was opened in October 1870 with twenty children. Admission was limited to two per family, nevertheless the demand rose rapidly and additional properties were obtained allowing 260 orphans to be housed. However, this still only covered one fifth of those needing help. Having charitable status, police contributions and public donations funded the orphanage until its closure in 1937.

Metropolitan and City Police Orphanage, Twickenham, The School Room.

SCHOOLING AT THE POLICE ORPHANAGE, c. 1904

The orphanage occupied a fifteen-acre site and had its own school, workshops, swimming pool, gymnasium, laundry and other amenities. The institution was all embracing, had a fine academic record, a distinctive uniform and their own school magazine. Discipline was severe but pupils looked back with affection. Links were made with the Commonwealth and many of the pupils were assisted in emigrating to Australia, New Zealand and Canada where local police would assist in finding accommodation and employment and keep a fatherly eye well into the individuals maturing years.

POLICE SPORTS DAY

Fitness is an essential requirement of the police and to this end involvement in sporting activities is encouraged. Police sports days have always been part of the social calendar although it is unusual to see police officers taking part in full uniform. Five officers under an umpire's supervision are taking part in an undetermined activity but appearing to wrestle or unseat the constable from the wooden block. One officer appears to have a sheet of paper clenched in his mouth. At least they are seen to be enjoying themselves.

TUG OF WAR TEAM, HOVE, SUSSEX, JUNE 1909

Undoubtedly because of their stature and size the police teams excelled in the Tug of War events throughout the United Kingdom. Their expertise was such that the City of London team were World Champions, 1908. The Hove Police team were proud of their own record in the locality having been winners at the Tramway Sports at Southsea in June 1909.

SWIMMING CLUB 'N' DIVISION METROPOLITAN POLICE

Swimming was popular in the police service; there being the need for efficiency in swimming in the event of having to save life or effect a rescue from the water. It was also an individual pursuit allowing practice no matter what shift pattern the officer worked. The formation of clubs ensured business was mixed with pleasure and numerous inter-police and open events were staged. The 'N' division based in North London was very successful and are seen displaying their trophies and the star swimmers' vests adorned with medals.

HASTINGS AND ST. LEONARDS POLICE BAND

In the early 1900s most police forces at sometime had their own police band. Invariably the bandsmen were from within the ranks of the service with a number having had previous service in a military band. Like the Hastings and St. Leonards Police Band they were proud of their accomplishments playing locally in band concerts, processions and at major events. Such a band helped to break down any barrier between the local community and the police thereby cementing relationships and trust. Notice the maid at the window.

BIRMINGHAM CITY POLICE BAND, C. 1912

The forty-eight members of the Birmingham Police Band on parade for a photo-call by the bandstand in a Birmingham Park. Brass, wind and string instruments are on display allowing a wide range of music to be played. The larger forces often had smaller divisional bands that could either operate separately or be combined into a central band. The West Midlands Police Force continue to entertain the people of Birmingham having both a brass band and a pipe band.

HIS MAJESTY'S INSPECTOR OF CONSTABULARY, NORWICH, 1919

A December inspection is in progress with the Chief Constable, John Dain, escorting His Majesty's Inspector of Constabulary through the ranks of the force. The Home Secretary obtained power to appoint Inspectors of Constabulary in 1856. Since that time forces have been visited every year and inspected to assess their state and efficiency. Without their satisfactory report, the Home Secretary could withhold the Home Office financial grant. H.M. Inspectors are not police officers and do not have the status of constable. It is customary to appoint persons with considerable experience in the office of chief constable to the post.

HAMPSHIRE POLICE IN ODIHAM, c. 1904

The sergeant and constables of Odiham, Hampshire stage a scene for a local photographer reverting back to the earlier punishment of the stocks. Note the distinctive light coloured braiding to the epaulettes and collar. The stocks were a centuries old punishment having been used for the hooligans and minor criminals of the day. The use of stocks, although never abolished, gradually ceased during the nineteenth century with the possible last recorded case being in 1865 at Rugby.

VILLAGE LOCK-UP, c. 1900

Prior to the formation of the modern police,a parish constable was in many instances provided with a village lock-up to house prisoners. Several of these remain and can be seen on village greens and other prominent places. On the formation of police forces, the constables in rural areas had difficulty in housing and handling prisoners. Often there was no transport readily available to convey prisoners to Police Stations and officially provided cells. Consequently they had to find methods of securing prisoners by chaining or finding locked accommodation and, as a result, it was not unknown for the village lock-up still to be used for the purpose.

IMPERSONATING A POLICE OFFICER, BIRMINGHAM, 1901

It is an offence to impersonate a police officer, however, this did not stop David Lloyd George, then a young Liberal pro-Boer orator in 1901. The Tories supported the British action against the Boers in South Africa together with the majority of the uninformed populace. The Colonial Minister, Joseph Chamberlain, was a native of Birmingham hence when Lloyd George spoke he enraged the locals who stormed the Town Hall, broke doors and windows and fought with the police. Shots were fired with one man killed and 97 policemen injured. For his own safety Lloyd George escaped through a back door disguised as a policeman.

CLAVERING MURDER, ESSEX

Samuel Herbert Dougal being escorted from Moat Farm, Clavering, Essex on the 30th April, 1903. He was charged with the murder of Miss Camille Holland on or about the 19th May, 1899 by Detective Inspector Marden of the Essex Police. Dougal had met Holland in London and using her money had bought the farm. Within three weeks he had shot and killed her, burying her in a farm ditch. Forgeries then came to light in 1902 and during enquiries suspicions were raised and the farm searched. The body was eventually found and in due course Dougal was found guilty and hanged on the 14th July, 1903.

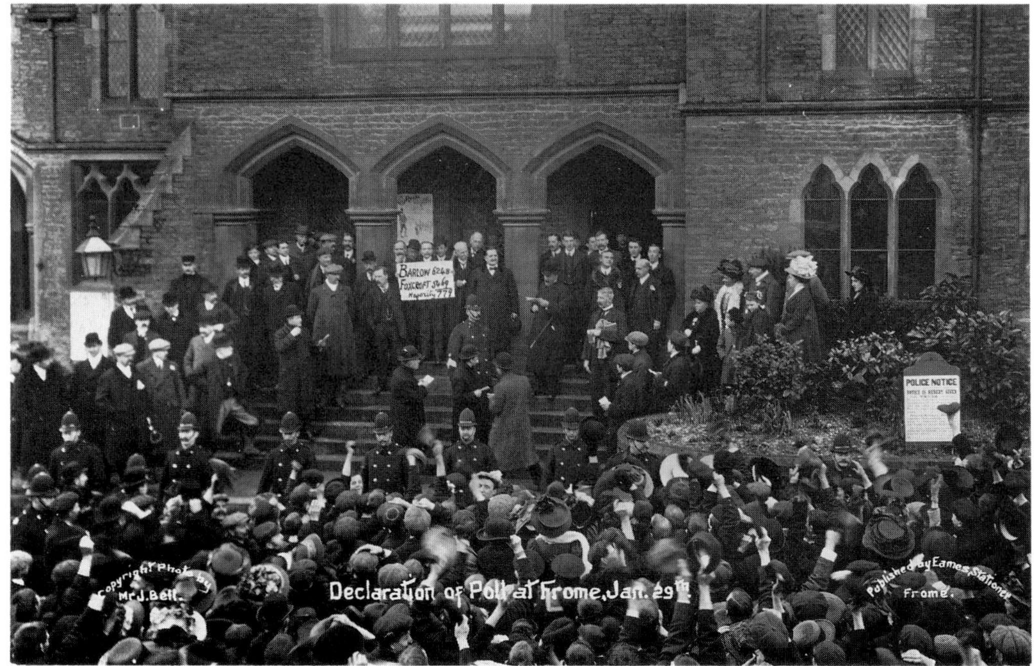

ELECTION DUTY, FROME, SOMERSET, 10th JANUARY 1910

Police have always held an important role at times of a General Election. They are required to ensure free access to polling stations and maintain order if required. They supervise the security of the voting boxes and the count, and as at Frome are present in numbers at the time of the declaration of the result. On this occasion a victory for the Liberal candidate, Sir John Barlow.

FIREARM AT THE READY, 1940

It has always been a proud fact that the British Police Force is basically an unarmed service relying on experience, persuasion and goodwill to maintain effective policing. The effect of the Sidney Street Siege, the requirements of wartime and the need to protect royalty and statesmen meant that some officers had to be experienced in the use of firearms. Today the wider availability and greater criminal use of firearms has resulted in all forces having a specialised firearms group, nevertheless the overall position is that the carrying of firearms is rare, officers still relying on their authority and the truncheon for protection.

RETIREMENT PRESENTATION, c. 1910

A fine body of 'L' Division officers, London, pose for the presentation photograph for what is undoubtedly a reitrement occasion. As well as detectives on the back row, off-duty colleagues, one having brought his son, having returned to wish the recipient well. The chiming clock will remind him that after 30 years of shift work he can now anticipate more regular hours and a less disciplined life style.

POLICEMAN'S WEDDING DAY, DOVER, c. 1912

This couple leave the church to be met by a guard of honour formed by colleagues in the Dover Police. What better way to make the triumphal arch then with raised truncheons. But even marriage was not a straight forward decision as the officer had to submit his bride's name to his force for clearance and permission to marry. She would also become subject to the restrictions placed on a policeman's domestic life.

AN ARRESTING ASSIGNMENT

Proving the point that some police duty is enjoyable, two Hampshire constables are seen taking good care of Miss World 1988, Linda Petursdottir from Iceland, at the Chineham Centre, Basingstoke.